The Reporter's Notebook

—

Writing Tools
for Student Journalists

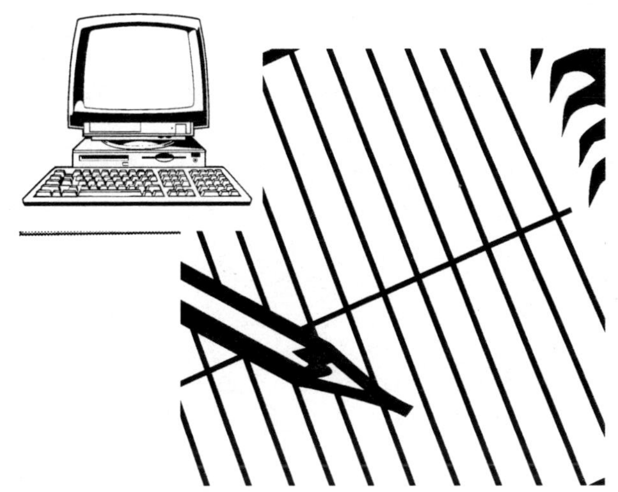

Mark Levin

Mind-Stretch Publishing

The Reporter's Notebook
—
Writing Tools
for Student Journalists

by
Mark Levin

published by
Mind-Stretch Publishing
3124 Landrum Road
Columbus, NC 28722
828/863-4235
www.mindstretch.com

ISBN-13: 978-0-9676409-0-7
ISBN-10: 0-9676409-0-3

Printed in the United States of America
by Morris Publishing • 3212 East Highway 30
Kearney, NE 68847

20 19 18 17 16 15 14 13

The Reporter's Notebook

____

Name of Reporter

____

Name of Newspaper

____

Name of School

____

Street Address

____

City, State, ZIP

____

Phone

____

School Year

Table of Contents

Advice from the Pros —

How to Use
The Reporter's Notebook
an introduction

Whether you are an experienced student journalist or a cub reporter, you will find plenty of helpful information, advice, planning forms, and more to get and keep you organized.

The first part of this notebook contains the tools of the trade. Each new tool will have a short explanation to help you get started. You should explore each of these sections to see just what is there and how you will be able to make the most of this information.

The second part of *The Reporter's Notebook* is where you will craft your stories. Use these pages to brainstorm story ideas, to write down interview questions, to outline your stories, and to sketch out your rough drafts. Throughout this section you will find bits of advice to student writers from a variety of well-known professional writers and journalists. I hope these words of wisdom from those who have paid their dues will help motivate you to be the best writer that you can be.

Don't forget to record your accomplishments as you set about this business of journalism this year. You will even find a page for that.

Best wishes as you begin this journey. If you think of new pages that should be added to future editions of *The Reporter's Notebook*, please let me know. And I would love to see some of your published work.

—*Mark Levin*

Journalism Basics 101
a little journalism info
all reporters should know

Remember that the **First Amendment** to the United States Constitution protects the right of journalists to report the news. Our Founding Fathers went to war to protect this right. Treat it carefully through fair, complete, and accurate reporting.

Journalists answer questions and sometimes entertain. Occasionally this happens together, though often stories written for different purposes are written in different styles. Make sure you know who your readers will be for a particular story.

The 5 Ws and 1 H

All news stories need to answer the questions of:

Who?•What?•Where?•When?•Why?•& How?

After you have roughed out your story, go back through and make sure you have answered these questions. If you have left something out, get it answered. One point to keep in mind — some of these questions might be more important than others. Emphasize those.

The Inverted Pyramid Style of Writing

In most news stories, the important information comes first. If a reader only gets through the first half of a story, you can at least feel satisfied knowing that you got your message across — even if not a complete one.

Did you Know? In the days when type had to be set by hand, editors loved to cut stories by removing words from the bottom. This saved a typesetter from having to reset entire stories — another reason reporters wrote using the Inverted Pyramid. Today, with computer layout, this is history.

Some Basic Steps to Follow in Writing Stories

1. Start with your story assignment. Think about how you will approach it. What is your news angle? Will this be *straight* (hard) news or a *feature* (soft) news? Make sure your story passes the "who cares" test. If you feel no one will be interested in what you are about to write, then you either need to choose another topic or write it so that people *do* care.

2. Smart research is next. Find out all you can about your subject. This will lead to good interview questions. Avoid questions that will end in only "yes" or "no" answers.

3. Decide what the main point is that you want to make. (This might help you write an attention-getting lead.) This is sometimes called the *nut graph,* because it is the point of the story in a nutshell.

4. Before starting your rough draft, outline what you want to say. Organize your paragraphs so that the reader has an easier time understanding what you are trying to get across.

5. Write your rough draft. Read it aloud. Does it make sense both ways?

6. Fine-tune the story. Cuts words if you need to. Add details if you have not answered all of the 5 Ws and H.

7. Verify facts, check quotes.

8. If you haven't already written a good lead — do so. The lead needs to entice your readers into reading the whole story. A good lead at least makes sure they will start.

9. Add a headline if you are required to do so. Make it active by using a verb.

10. Edit and proofread and edit and proofread.

Basic Journalism Vocabulary

There are lots of words journalists should have in their vocabulary. These are some of the "must knows."

angle — how you approach the story.

attribution — a statement that says where you got your information.

banner — a large headline that extends across a page, used for very important information.

beat — the regular area of news that a reporter covers.

byline — who wrote the story.

copy — the actual text of a story.

cutline/caption — an explanation of a photo or other graphic.

dateline — the line at the beginning of a story that names the origin of the story.

edit — to make changes to a story to help clarity. May include cutting or adding to a story.

editorial — a story that expresses an opinion.

feature (soft news) — a story that captures more of the human interest angle. It may not be as timely as hard or straight news.

graphic — everything that isn't copy, including photos, graphs, drawings, line art.

hard news (straight news) — news that reports just the facts. Is usually more timely than feature news.

headline — the title of the story.

lead — the opening sentence or paragraph.

libel — damaging someone's reputation by what you print.

masthead — where all the important publication information about the newspaper is printed.

nameplate (flag) — the title of the newspaper in large letters on the front page.

proofing — the process of going through a story word for word, line by line, looking for mechanical errors.

stylebook (or style sheet) — rules for a newspaper's system of grammar, punctuation, and usage, as well as requirements such as margin dimensions and which fonts are used.

Future Book

Record all known events here for the upcoming year. Use your school's yearly calendar to get started. Add events as you find out about them. These events can lead to stories, and by knowing what is ahead — you will be able to write more timely stories.

August_______________________________________

____

____

September_______________________________________

____

____

October_______________________________________

____

____

November_______________________________________

____

____

December_______________________________________

____

____

January

February

March

April

May

June

July

Ten Ways to Find Stories

contributed by Michele Dunaway

1. Use a beat system. Each student should be assigned a teacher who they visit with on a regular basis.

2. Walk the hallways. Just what *is* going on in your school?

3. Use a story tip sheet. This is a sheet non-journalism students pick up at a central location on which they write down their story ideas.

4. Watch the local news. Just what is going on in your town that can be covered by localizing it to your school?

5. Watch the national news. Just what is going on in the nation and world that concerns students?

6. Create a story idea bank. Brainstorm for 10 minutes, thinking of all the story ideas you can use.

7. Think sports/clubs/activities. What do kids want to know about — that isn't old news?

8. Think issues. What can be localized to your school?

9. Ask! Ask! Go up to five people and ask them for ideas.

10. Keep your eyes and ears open. Quite often a story idea is right under your nose. It is so obvious that everyone misses it.

Story Ideas

Use these pages to start brainstorming your story ideas. Record them. Be creative. Think of stories that have never been covered before and of ways to transform old stories into fresh ideas. Remember that one idea can lead to 10 others.

1.____

2.____

3.____

4.____

5.____

6.____

7.____

8.____

9.____

10.____

11.____

12.____

13.____

14.____

15.____

Story Ideas Bank

contributed by Marilyn Eckels & Pat Hinman

Still can't think of anything to write about? These ideas should get you started.

- Making Excuses
- Staying Home Alone
- Early Rising
- Lockers — Clean, Messy, Aggravations
- Backpack Stories/Stuff
- Weekend Activities
- Exceptionally Talented Students
- Bus Riding/Getting to School
- Bubble Gum
- Glasses, Contacts, Braces
- Snow/Weather
- Babysitting
- Embarrassing Moments
- Dyeing Hair
- Communication/Telephone/Internet/Passing Notes
- Trends and Fads
- Parent-Kid Relationships
- Gossip
- Cafeteria — Seating, Food, etc.
- The Places You've Been/Visited, Lived, etc.
- Holidays
- Celebrating Birthdays
- TV Shows/Movies
- New Teachers
- What's In — What's Out
- Seeing Double — Twins
- Games Students Play
- Early Morning Routines
- Standing in Line
- School Spirit
- Brothers/Sisters in Same School

- Soap Opera Addiction
- Horoscopes
- Being an Only Child
- Students' Bedrooms
- Couch Potatoes
- Sports Outside the Spotlight
- Moving In, Moving Out
- Jobs, Chores at Homes
- Allowances
- Traveling with Family
- Living on the Edge — Doing Scary Things
- Coming to America as a Newcomer
- Being a Bookworm
- Superstitions
- Being Left-handed
- Being Very Tall or Very Short
- Staying at Home When You Are Sick
- Sleepovers
- Hobbies/Collections
- After-school Snacks
- Great Places to Visit that Only You Know About

Your Own Special Ideas—

____

____

____

____

____

____

____

What to Do
When You Have Writer's Block

Everyone has their own ideas about what works to get over writer's block. All writers have experienced moments when nothing seemed to *click*. Here are a few ideas that might help unclog your brain.

- Go someplace different. If you have been sitting at your desk, try going outside, to the library, to the cafeteria.

- Do some research. Perhaps you don't know where to start because you don't have enough background information.

- Forget about your assignment for a few minutes or even a day. Come back to it later.

- Try to mind-map your topic. Start with a key word in the center of a sheet of paper and branch off in any and all directions. Each of these branches could lead to a new story idea.

- Pick a different time of day to write.

- Look through books and magazines for ideas.

- Sit and observe what's around you. An idea might come to you.

- Make lists. For starters begin with things you know a lot about and then add things you would like to learn about. You might possibly find a story here.

- Write anything. Don't worry if it's on your topic.

Upcoming Deadlines

Use this section to keep track of important dates associated with each of your articles.

Article Assigned____

For Issue Dated____

Interview Deadline____

Rough Draft Deadline____

Final Copy Deadline____

Notes:____

____

____

Article Assigned____

For Issue Dated____

Interview Deadline____

Rough Draft Deadline____

Final Copy Deadline____

Notes:____

____

____

Article Assigned____

For Issue Dated____

Interview Deadline____

Rough Draft Deadline____

Final Copy Deadline____

Notes:____

____

____

____

____

Article Assigned____

For Issue Dated____

Interview Deadline____

Rough Draft Deadline____

Final Copy Deadline____

Notes:____

____

____

Article Assigned______________________________________

For Issue Dated______________________________________

Interview Deadline____________________________________

Rough Draft Deadline__________________________________

Final Copy Deadline___________________________________

Notes:____

____

____

____

____

Article Assigned______________________________________

For Issue Dated______________________________________

Interview Deadline____________________________________

Rough Draft Deadline__________________________________

Final Copy Deadline___________________________________

Notes:____

____

____

____

Scheduled Interview Reminders
idea contributed by Brad Kuhns

Use this section to remind you of all the details associated with an interview.

Interview With______________________________

For article about______________________________

Day and Date of Interview______________________________

Time of Interview______________________________

Place______________________________

_______ Check when interview questions are written

_______ Check if camera or photographer needed

Interview With______________________________

For article about______________________________

Day and Date of Interview______________________________

Time of Interview______________________________

Place______________________________

_______ Check when interview questions are written

_______ Check if camera or photographer needed

Interview With____

For article about_______________________________________

Day and Date of Interview_________________________________

Time of Interview_______________________________________

Place____

_____ Check when interview questions are written

_____ Check if camera or photographer needed

Notes:____

____

Interview With____

For article about_______________________________________

Day and Date of Interview_________________________________

Time of Interview_______________________________________

Place____

_____ Check when interview questions are written

_____ Check if camera or photographer needed

Notes:____

____

Interview With____

For article about____

Day and Date of Interview_________________________________

Time of Interview____

Place____

_____ Check when interview questions are written

_____ Check if camera or photographer needed

Notes:____

____

Interview With____

For article about____

Day and Date of Interview_________________________________

Time of Interview____

Place____

_____ Check when interview questions are written

_____ Check if camera or photographer needed

Notes:____

____

Stock Interview Questions

Good interview questions make for good stories. Some interviews will be with people about other people or about events and happenings. Other interviews will be biographical, where you are interviewing the person about himself or herself.

You should spend time researching your story and writing questions before ever going out on an interview. If you really get stuck for a beginning, use the following ideas to help get you started. These questions are for biographical interviews.

- Who influenced you the most?

- When were you the happiest, saddest?

- If you could start over, how would you change things?

- How would others describe you?

- For what do you want to be remembered?

- What do you hope to be doing 10 years from now?

- How would you change things about this school?

- What would you like readers to know about you?

- What advice would you like to give?

- What has been the hardest obstacle you've had to overcome to get to where you are today?

- If you could thank one person right now for helping you out of some tough situation, who would it be?

Interviewing Checklist

Before going on your interview, make sure you have completed the following items. You might want to make copies of this page for each interview, or just make a mental check before heading out the door.

_____ Interview scheduled

_____ Questions written (at least 10 *good* questions)

_____ Arrangements have been made to get you to your interview

_____ Camera loaded and you know how to use it, or

_____ Photographer arrangements made

To Take With You—

_____ Reporter's Notebook (and possibly a recorder)

_____ Pens/pencils & press badge and other credentials

_____ Camera (or photographer)

During & After the Interview —

_____ Read back all quotes for accuracy

_____ Ask for exact spelling of all names

_____ Send a copy of the rough draft if asked

_____ Send a copy of the published story along with a note of thanks

Editing Checklist

Use this form as a final check for each of your
articles. You should make copies of this blank form
to use throughout the year.

Article Headline____

Is this headline interesting and catchy?

Does this headline relate to the story?

Is my lead interesting?

Will people want to read my story?

Have I answered each of the following questions:
Who?
What?
Where?
When?
Why?
How?

Does the article include good descriptions?

Have I checked all sources, quotes, facts? Are the
spellings of all names correct? Make sure to ask.

Have I read the entire story aloud?

Does each paragraph follow a logical order?

Is there a good ending?

Have I proofread this story closely?

Has someone else proofread and edited my story?

Commonly Misspelled Words

Your word processor will catch lots of mistakes, but it won't always know which word you meant to use. You should be familiar with all of these spelling nightmares.

accessory	forty	occasion	temporary
accommodate	gauge	occasionally	their
achievement	genuine	occurred	theory
acknowledge	gigantic	occurrence	tomorrow
a lot	gorgeous	opponent	twelfth
allotted	government	pamphlet	unanimous
all right	governor	parallel	usable
appearance	grammar	performance	vacuum
athletics	guarantee	permanent	vegetable
audible	guidance	perseverance	vicinity
auxiliary	gymnasium	persuade	volume
bicycle	height	physician	warranty
believable	hygiene	poison	Wednesday
business	illegible	possession	weight
calendar	immediately	privilege	weird
campaign	independence	procedure	yesterday
candidate	inflammable	proceed	youth
cemetery	irrelevant	professor	zealous
college	khaki	quantity	zoology
commitment	kindergarten	receive	
confident	knowledge	recommend	**Add your**
conscience	laboratory	relief	**own words**
conscientious	leisure	restaurant	**here:**
criticism	library	ridiculous	
deceive	maintenance	scholastic	
definite	mathematics	scissors	__________
development	mileage	secretary	
disappear	miscellaneous	separate	__________
embarrass	misspell	speech	
encyclopedia	nickel	succeed	__________
extraordinary	niece	suing	
familiar	nineteenth	superintendent	__________
February	ninety	surprise	
foreign	noticeable	temperature	__________

Top 10 Punctuation Tips
contributed by Claudia Sherry

1. Commas and periods *always* go inside quotation marks, whether or not they are a part of the quote.

2. Question marks, exclamation points, the dash, and the semi-colon go inside quotation marks *only if* they are part of the quote. Otherwise, place them outside the quotation.

3. Do not capitalize the seasons of the year or directional words (north, south, east, west). However, you should capitalize regions of the country:

   To get to the store, go south on Main Street.
   The Southwest doesn't get much rain.

4. Capitalize titles given in front of names, but not if used after the name to describe it:

   President Abraham Lincoln was a courageous man.
   Abraham Lincoln, the president during the Civil War, was a courageous man.
   Councilman Inman is coming to our school to speak.
   Mr. Inman, the councilman, will speak at our school this Friday.

5. Numbers from one to nine are normally written as words, whereas all double-digit numbers (10 and over) are written as numerals.
   However, if you are using two numbers together, they should be in the same style:

   We will see eight-ten new horses when we go to the stable today.

6. Never start a sentence with numerals:

   Twenty-five students went on the field trip.

7. If you are hand-writing a report, you underline book and other titles. However, you should *italicize* these titles when writing on the computer.

8. Hyphens are generally used with compound adjectives (two or more words that together describe the noun) if they precede the noun:

   She was wearing a bluish-green dress.
   L. J. Meyers scored a first-quarter goal.

9. Most combinations that are hyphenated before a noun are not hyphenated when they occur after the noun:

   Her dress was bluish green.
   He scored a goal in the first quarter of the game.
   However, there are some compound words that are always hyphenated, including any of the "self" words: *self-esteem, self-confidence, self-employed...*
   Other hyphenated compound words include: *great-grandmother, half-time, hands-on, well-known.*

When in doubt, check the dictionary!!

10. Do not use a hyphen to link the adverb *very* or for adverbs that end in *ly*:
    We have a very good time.
    "No running in the hallways" is an easily remembered rule.

Note: Your newspaper's particular stylebook may have slight variations on some of these tips.

Tips for Photographers

If you are responsible for taking the photos for your stories, keep these tips in mind.

• Make sure your camera has fresh batteries and your memory card has plenty of available space. Make sure you've practiced with the camera before going on assignment if it's not yours.

• Make sure your digital camera is set for a high resolution photo.

• Use the flash indoors (unless prohibited) and often outdoors to eliminate shadows.

• Come up close. Hold the camera steady.

• Take several photos of each subject and try different angles for more interesting shots.

• Avoid distracting backgrounds. Make sure you don't have trees or light poles growing out of someone's head.

• If you must take a photo of your subject against a reflective surface (glass, trophy case, etc.), shoot at a 45-degree angle to eliminate flash back.

• Have your subject in action doing something.

• If you must have a photo of a group of people, arrange them so that you can easily identify them in the caption. Go ahead and note the names in correct naming order when you take the photo.

Stylebook Reminders

Your newspaper will most likely have a published stylebook that will list just about every rule that has been established to help unify your publication.
Most of these rules relate to grammar, usage, and mechanics. Use the spaces here to record some of the specific layout formatting rules your newspaper may require.

Headlines —

Font____ Size____________

Copy —

Font____ Size____________

Cutlines/Captions —

Font____ Size____________

Margins —

Sizes___________________________________Right Justified?_____

Copy Writing:

How teachers are listed: *Mrs. Brown or Nancy Brown*

____

Other Reminders____

____

____

Contacts and Sources

Record the names, addresses, phone numbers, and any notes of people who have helped you with your stories. Include people you have interviewed, people you have used as sources, and people who you contact on your regular news beat. This information will come in handy when you need to call to ask a follow-up question or when you want to send a copy of your published story with a note of thanks.

Name_____________________________ Phone____________

Street Address____

City, State, ZIP____

Notes____

Name_____________________________ Phone____________

Street Address____

City, State, ZIP____

Notes____

Name_____________________________ Phone____________

Street Address____

City, State, ZIP____

Notes____

Name_______________________________ Phone_______________

Street Address____

City, State, ZIP____

Notes____

Name_______________________________ Phone_______________

Street Address____

City, State, ZIP____

Notes____

Name_______________________________ Phone_______________

Street Address____

City, State, ZIP____

Notes____

Name_______________________________ Phone_______________

Street Address____

City, State, ZIP____

Notes____

Name_______________________________ Phone_______________

Street Address____

City, State, ZIP____

Notes____

Name_________________________ Phone___________

Street Address____________________________________

City, State, ZIP___________________________________

Notes____

Name_________________________ Phone___________

Street Address____________________________________

City, State, ZIP___________________________________

Notes____

Name_________________________ Phone___________

Street Address____________________________________

City, State, ZIP___________________________________

Notes____

Name_________________________ Phone___________

Street Address____________________________________

City, State, ZIP___________________________________

Notes____

Name_________________________ Phone___________

Street Address____________________________________

City, State, ZIP___________________________________

Notes____

My Personal Best

Record your journalistic achievements for the year here. This information might help you later when you decide to take your writing to the next level.

People I Have Interviewed —

who   date

who   date

who   date

who   date

who   date

Stories I Have Had Published —

headline   publication   date

headline   publication   date

headline   publication   date

headline   publication   date

headline	publication	date

headline	publication	date

headline	publication	date

headline	publication	date

Awards and Honors —

name of award	date

name of award	date

name of award	date

Staff Positions I Have Held —

position	date

position	date

Notes:

Journalism Resources

Reference Books (available in your school library)

Encyclopedias (hard-copy editions as well as CD-ROM and web based) — essential to starting your research on almost any topic.

World Almanacs — great place to find up-to-date facts about a variety of information such as the most popular movies at the box office last year.

Magazines and Newspapers — will provide information about current events. It's important to have access to the *Readers Guide to Periodical Literature* to research particular topics.

Phone Books — where you might need to start to get information for a local story.

Dictionary and Thesaurus — critical tools for checking spellings and meanings, and for finding better words.

Organizations

National Elementary Schools Press Association
Carolina Day School
1345 Hendersonville Road
Asheville, NC 28803
828/ 274-0758 X818 • www.nespa.org

Offers help for both elementary and middle schools. Provides a student recognition service and a rating and review program.

Journalism Education Association
Kansas State University, 103 Kedzie Hall
Manhattan, KS 66506
785/ 532-5532 • www.jea.org

Offers programs for both students and advisers,
including an awards program and teacher
certification. They publish a great catalog of
journalism-related books.

Student Press Law Center
1815 N. Fort Myer Drive, Suite 800
Arlington, VA 22209
703/ 807-1904 • www.splc.org

The SPLC offers information and legal help regarding
the media for students and their advisers.

The Writing Company
P. O. Box 802
Culver City, CA 90232-0802
800-421-4246

This company has great catalogs on journalism and
writing books and resources.

Other Publishing Books by Mark Levin —
(*Kids in Print* and *Real World Writing Opportunities* are available
through Mind-Stretch. Order form on page 99.)

Kids in Print — Publishing A School Newspaper
©1997 Good Apple/Frank Schaffer

Real World Writing Opportunities for Kids
©2000 Good Apple/Frank Schaffer

EXp3: Journalism — A Handbook for Journalists
©2000 National Textbook Company/NTC
Contemporary Publishers — 800-323-4900

Notes

____

____

____

____

____

____

____

____

____

Advice from the Pros—

"Check and double-check your facts. There is no place for the question mark or unanswered questions on the written page. Also, persevere. You'll find that the competition isn't as intense as you might imagine — because so many are so willing to drop out of the race."

—*Marilyn Beck*

Marilyn Beck is a syndicated entertainment columnist in Hollywood.

Advice from the Pros—

"Always remember that the best way to learn to write is to read. The next best way to learn to write is to write and write, and write some more. There really are no short cuts."

—Frank DeFord

Frank DeFord is Senior Contributing Editor for *Sports Illustrated* and a regular correspondent on National Public Radio. He has written a dozen books.

Advice from the Pros—

"In an era of increasing impersonality, a journalist does his or her work today and sees the product of it tomorrow — with his or her name on it. That's more important than wealth, and will be even more so in years to come."

—*Tom Wicker*

Tom Wicker is an author and a retired columnist for *The New York Times*.

____

____

____

____

____

____

____

____

____

Advice from the Pros—

"If I could give young people one piece of advice, it would be, read, read, read! In reading, you will open up new worlds, real and imagined. Read for information, read for pleasure. Our libraries are filled with knowledge and joy, and it's all there — free for the taking. The person who *does not* read is no better off than the person who *cannot* read."

—*Abigail Van Buren*

Abigail Van Buren is known to her millions of readers as *Dear Abby*. According to *Editor & Publisher's* recent figures, her advice column is the most widely syndicated column in the world.

____

____

____

____

____

____

____

____

Advice from the Pros—

"It's important to know for whom you are
writing. When I was a kid, and started submitting
freelance articles on spec, I made the mistake of
sending the same piece to a variety of magazines.
Every publication has a specific audience — and, for
the most part, a specific attitude. Your work can still
be as personal as you want it to be, but if you
haven't tailored your thoughts for the specific
readers you want to reach, you are doing both
yourself and them a great disservice."

—*Leonard Maltin*

Leonard Maltin is a TV interviewer/commentator, film critic and
essayist. He sold his first article at the age of 13 and had his
first book published at 18. His annual paperback *Leonard
Maltin's Movie and Video Guide* has become a standard work for
buffs and professionals alike.

____

____

____

____

____

____

____

____

____

____

Advice from the Pros—

"The key to success is to make everybody in the class laugh. It may not go over well with the teachers, but when you grow up and make a fortune they will claim you were one of them."

—*Art Buchwald*

Art Buchwald was a syndicated columnist for *The Los Angeles Times* and the author of over 30 books. Mr. Buchwald was a recipient of the Pulitzer Prize and was elected to the American Academy of Arts and Letters. He died in January 2007.

____

____

____

____

____

____

____

____

____

Advice from the Pros—

"My main advice to young journalists is to have an open mind and an eager curiosity about everything. You must have an enthusiasm for work; if not, get out of the business."

—*Clifton Daniel*

Clifton Daniel served in several positions at *The New York Times* including editor. The biggest story he ever covered was the dropping of the atom bomb during World World II. He has received the Overseas Press Club award for his reporting, among others. Mr. Daniel died on February 21, 2000, a few months after contributing this bit of advice.

____

____

____

____

____

____

____

____

____

____

Advice from the Pros—

"Be truthful and accurate, but remember: reporting the facts is anybody's job. Writing with an extra dash of spice, selecting the most interesting descriptive words and pruning away the clutter, is what is known as style. It's the thing that separates the successes from the also-rans."

—*Rex Reed*

Rex Reed is the author of nine books and hundreds of articles, a film critic, and a journalist.

____

____

____

____

____

____

____

____

Advice from the Pros—

"I feel anyone who has something to say is a writer. It's our desire to communicate an experience which brings out the writer in us. What's the best way to find interesting stories? Just talk with people. Everybody has an interesting story to share. Writing is hard work. Just because it doesn't come easily, doesn't mean that you're not a good writer, or that you don't have something valid to say. Getting your thoughts into the written word can be a mentally painful process. With practice and patience, anyone can learn how to write."

—*Jane Miller*

Jane Miller is a free-lance writer. Her works appears regularly in *The Pittsburgh Post-Gazette.*

———————————————————————

———————————————————————

———————————————————————

———————————————————————

———————————————————————

———————————————————————

———————————————————————

———————————————————————

———————————————————————

———————————————————————

Advice from the Pros—

"Read everything, but make up your own mind. And never take authority figures too seriously."

—*Dave Barry*

Dave Barry is an author and a humor columnist for *The Miami Herald.* He is a winner of the Pulitzer Prize.

Advice from the Pros—

"Work on your school paper. Work hard."
—*John Stossel*

John Stossel is a television correspondent for ABC News.

____

____

____

____

____

____

____

____

____

Advice from the Pros—

"You never know when you're going to come across a great story idea. Before I begin a book, I fill a whole notebook. So, carry a small notebook with you and jot down everything you see and hear — bits of dialogue, ideas for scenes, background information, descriptions of people and places, details, and more details.

But, even with my notebook, I still don't know everything. For me, finding out is the best part of writing."

—*Judy Blume*

Judy Blume is a popular author of books for children, young adults, and their parents.

Advice from the Pros—

"Write! Write every day, until it becomes second nature to you. Keep a journal. Write letters to the editor. Participate in online discussion groups. Use e-mail. And…read even more than you write."

—*Roger Ebert*

Roger Ebert is a syndicated film critic for *The Chicago Sun-Times*. He is a winner of the Pulitzer Prize.

____

____

____

____

____

____

____

____

____

Advice from the Pros—

"Newspaper work requires an interesting mix of personalities and talents. To put out a good newspaper, of any size, you must first assemble that mix of talents, and then you must get them working together as a team."

—*Jeff Byrd*

Jeff Byrd is editor and publisher of the *Tryon Daily Bulletin*, Tryon, North Carolina, the world's smallest daily newspaper.

____

____

____

____

____

____

____

____

____

____

Advice from the Pros—

"Reading is the greatest gift a person can give oneself. It is also a great adventure. Reading can take you to faraway places, and introduce you to new and exciting cultures and people. Reading a lot will open your mind and your world, and it gives you something no one can ever take away — knowledge. So be adventurous and read, read, read!"

—*Connie Chung*

Connie Chung is a veteran broadcast journalist, currently with ABC News. She has won three Emmy Awards.

Advice from the Pros—

"Your mission (if you choose to accept it) is to help recover the reputation of the press. So, young TV reporter, don't poke your microphone in the face of the person on the stretcher and ask how it felt when the plane crashed. Young investigator, be careful of the friendly but nameless official who has a scoop for you. Young police reporter, watch out for the law enforcement officer who has an inside tip on the *real* guilty person. And producers, remember that people are persons, not *generic footage*. A little respect for privacy."

—*Daniel Schorr*

Daniel Schorr is a news analyst for National Public Radio. He has received numerous awards and foreign decorations, but declares his greatest moment was appearing as Number 17 on President Nixon's *Enemies List.*

———————————————————————

———————————————————————

———————————————————————

———————————————————————

———————————————————————

———————————————————————

———————————————————————

———————————————————————

———————————————————————

———————————————————————

Advice from the Pros—

"My advice for foreign correspondents is: Never go into a country where the biggest story to come out would be your death."

—*David Zucchino*

David Zucchino is a foreign correspondent for *The Philadelphia Inquirer*. He won a Pulitzer Prize for his reporting from South Africa.

Acknowledgements

The author wishes to thank the following for their contributions and assistance.

Claudia Sherry, Editor
Lower School Head
Carolina Day School
Asheville, North Carolina

Michele Dunaway
Language Arts/Journalism Teacher
Rockwood South Middle School
Fenton, Missouri

Marilyn Eckels & Pat Hinman
Journalism Advisers
Robinson Middle School
Fairfax, Virginia

Brad Kuhns
Student Consultant
Carolina Day School
Asheville, North Carolina

Jane Miller
Free-lance Columnist
The Pittsburgh Post-Gazette
Pittsburgh, Pennsylvania

Mind-Stretch Publishing

Mind-Stretch Order Form

To order additional copies of *The Reporter's Notebook* or other Mind-Stretch books, complete the information below:

Ship to: (please print)

Name____

Address____

City, State ZIP_______________________________________

Day Phone____

Email____

______copies of *The Reporter's Notebook* @ $10

______copies of *Kids in Print—Publishing A School Newspaper-Second Edition* @ $15

______copies of *Real-World Writing Opportunities for Kids* @ $15

______copies of *Team Building Made Easy* @ $12

Total of Order $_______________

Postage/handling by U.S. Priority Mail
$4.85 first 2 books, $1 each extra book) $_______________

NC residents add sales tax $_______________

Total amount enclosed $_______________

Make checks payable to **Mind-Stretch** and mail to:
Mind-Stretch, 3124 Landrum Road, Columbus, NC 28722
828/ 863-4235   www.mindstretch.com

Got Ideas?

Now that you've used this first edition of *The Reporter's Notebook*, send us your ideas for the second edition. We'll list your name as a contributor if we use your great idea. Send to our address on the order form found on the reverse side.

____

____

____

____

____

____

____

____

____

Don't forget —

Name____

Address_____________________________________

City, State, ZIP____________________________